AS CONSTANT AS TIME
MY LOVELY GIRL.
LETS RUN A
AND EDINBURGH

10 FILMS
WITH MY
DAD

BY
AIDAN GOATLEY

KIMBLE PUBLISHING

ISBN 978-1-291-21907-4

90000

9 781291 219074

CHAPTERS

'FANTASTIC' 'CHARMING' 'DELIGHTFUL'
★★★★ ★★★★★ ★★★★
Three Weeks   Borderlines Film Festival   Latest 7

AIDAN GOATLEY
10 FILMS WITH MY DAD

A STAND UP COMEDY SHOW FOR ANYONE WHO'S EVER HAD A DAD

'A LOVELY LITTLE SHOW. TAKE YOUR DAD'
Kate Copstick- The Scotsman

'HIGHLY ENJOYABLE'
-The Skinny

'VERY, VERY FUNNY'
- edfringe.com

'A HEART-WARMING STORY ABOUT COMMUNICATION'
- Three Weeks

'GREAT COMEDY THAT POKES FUN AT HOLLYWOOD ICONS'
-Borderlines Film Festival

2:40PM Voodoo Rooms V68
4-25th AUGUST NOT 14TH

Λ.

CHAPTER 1
THE GREATEST STORY EVER TOLD

This is a story about communication. It's about how my Dad & I never talked.

We only ever watched films.

It's ok though, there is a happy ending so stick with it. This isn't going to be several hours' worth of reading followed by a massive downer of regret and lost opportunities.

I hate that.

Nothing gets me more riled than a good story spoiled at the end by a depressing ending. Like *'The Departed.'* 2 hours I sat through the film and in the end everyone dies except Mark Wahlberg and an obvious visual rat metaphor.

How can this be? Don't get me wrong. I don't mind bad guys winning or good guys being a little rough around the edges, it's just that I love films. It was how I was brought up. Consequently I just get angry if the love I've given these characters is just thrown away at the end leaving a sweary Mark Wahlberg. (This may not happen that often but we can only hope that *'Transformers 4'* has a similar ending.)

Also, it doesn't go on too long. It hasn't been strung out so that it can be extended into a trilogy. If, like me, you thought *'Lord of The Rings'* was a nine hour film about walking and sat there thinking 'Why didn't they just take the giant eagles to Mount Doom? There are giant eagles. Where did they keep the giant eagles? FRICKIN GIANT EAGLES!" then this should be for you.

Also, no one dies at the end and most importantly of all none of it is in 3D.

I guess I'm trying to say I hope you'll enjoy the story because nearly all of it is true and it's like a movie but in paper form.

I guess the root of our communication problems was a generational one. Dad was born in 1941 during World War 2 when men were 'MEN.'
I was born in 1971. When men had long hair, wore flares and were obsessed by fondue. It was also a time where men thought that Freddy Mercury was just a little bit flamboyant.
Not Dad. Dad had been a chief engineer in the navy and had undoubtedly encountered many flamboyant men in his time.
It may seem silly now but life was not as free (not that it still couldn't use a bit more freedom) as it is now. We had no idea. Yeah, he was a little bit camp but he was a rock god. When he finally came out, sadly days before his death, most people were shocked. The same can be said of Elton John. ('But he married Rene!' said a distraught Elton fancying female friend)
This is what we project and want in our stars. We want the chance,

however slight, we may be able to be with or know them in some way more than on our screen. This is the immediacy of modern media. We see them right there on the screen so often we feel as if we know them. Consequently we project our own beliefs on them and when we read that Gwyneth Paltrow has split with Brad Pitt it won't be long before she's ringing your doorbell. (Curse that Chris Martin for getting in the way)

In the 70's attitudes to different lifestyles were sadly not as advanced as they are now. Consequently Dad's biggest fear when I was born was that I would grow up to be gay.

I should in all honesty tell you that I now live in Brighton, considered by many to be the gay capital of the world. Think San Francisco but without the Bridge.

However, I am not gay. I just like to annoy dad.

Even in Brighton homophobia sadly still exists.

I have a little dog called Masie and an

8-year-old daughter, so everything has to be pink. One morning I was out walking my little dog with her pink lead when I bumped into a man. I apologised. He looked at me. Looked at the dog. Noted her lead & collar, then looked back at me.

'Gay!" he sneered.

Now you know in life when you think of a suitable response but it's usually 24 hours later? This was the first time I'd ever thought of one straightaway.

I looked at him in shock.

Looked at the dog.

Looked back at him and said,

"I don't know. I've never asked her before?"

And then I punched the bigot in the face and ran way. (I didn't of course. I'm middle-class and live in the centre of Brighton. Instead I walked away and wrote a pithy joke about it, then sat down and had some gluten free focaccia with red pepper hummus.)

Back in 1971 Dad had a plan to ensure my masculinity.

It was a 2-fold plan. First he would

make sure I watched every single John Wayne film ever made & secondly he would buy me weapons. Lots of weapons.

There was a boy called Chris Hardy, who lived ten doors up from us, was only 2 months older than me and for his 5th birthday he got a Grifter bicycle. It was awesome. It was the pinnacle of technology and above all else it was cool. It was the coolest thing ever made. It was brown, (this was the 70's, everything brown was cool, even pants) had gold flames on the bodywork and I wanted one.

I wanted one like I had never wanted anything before in my life.

So I started my campaign. Being 5 years old my campaign quickly degenerated to begging constantly day & night for it.

"Can I get a Grifter?"

"Eat your breakfast"

"Can I get a Grifter?"

"Put your seatbelt on."

"Can I get a Grifter?"

"Eat your dinner."

"Can I get a Grifter?"

"FOR THE LOVE OF ALL THINGS HOLY CAN YOU AT LEAST STOP TO BREATHE?"

Surely 2 months of constant begging would result in meeting my goal? What I didn't know was that Dad had already analyzed the situation.

You see, as an engineer his brain works in a very specific controlled manner. He will look at any situation and apply strict controlled questions and several laws of physics to get his answer. Also the fact that he knows absolutely everything there is to know about everything is a factor.

This had helped him to rise to the level of Chief Engineer, that and shouting a lot. I don't mean in an aggressive way at all, it's just that my father is exceptionally English and is therefore exceptionally loud in a way that only exceptionally English men can be.

I remember when we went to America and we were sat right at the back of the plane. My father gave me a quick lesson on flight engineering by whispering in my ear,

"THOSE WINGS WILL MOVE AT LEAST EIGHT FEET UP & DOWN DURING FLIGHT BUT WILL BE UNDER THE MOST STRESS DURING TAKE OFF. NOW THE ADVANTAGE OF US BEING AT THE BACK MEANS THAT IF WE BREAK UP ON TAKE OFF. FROM HERE, WE'LL HAVE THE BEST VIEW!"

Never boring traveling with my Dad and you usually get to meet the Air Marshall.

When I woke up on that morning I didn't know that my father had already checked out the Grifter bicycle and had found it to be unsuitable for purpose (a fact borne out as the Grifter was notoriously heavy, lacked any suspension and would be soon overtaken by the far popular BMX style of bikes) so he had made other purchases. On July 13th 1976 while Chris Hardy was undoubtedly hugging his Grifter I went down stairs to discover that Dad had bought me an air rifle and a hunting knife.

He bought his 5 year old what would now be described as offensive weapons. This was the 70's in a time before health & safety executives had taken over. I was lucky Dad hadn't bought me a nuclear bomb,

"YOU SEE SON THIS IS THE ADVANTAGE OF HAVING A ONE MEGATON DEVICE. IT'S EASY TO TRANSPORT AND COMES EQUIPPED WITH A FULL PRIMING KIT. NOW OFF YOU GO AND PLAY."

Dad was very excited and quickly set up a target on one of the trees in the back garden and filmed me on his Super 8 camera as I manfully popped away at the target.

15 years later the tree died of lead poisoning. Mother was furious and accused me. I in turn blamed dad so he dug out the old Super 8 film and like some bizarre homage to Kevin Costner in JFK acted as prosecutor in my trial.

"AND HERE WE CAN CLEARLY SEE AIDAN SHOOTING THE

TREE. AND THE TREE MOVES BACK AND TO THE LEFT. BACK AND TO THE LEFT. BACK AND TO THE LEFT."

When I wasn't destroying the environment we would watch films. This was a glorious time for watching films on TV in the years before soap operas took over the schedules and it took ages for films to emerge onto our screens. There were only three channels (BBC1, BBC2 and ITV) they only started at 12pm and showed old films by the bucket load.

Dad would sit me and my sister down and watch every classic film we could. From black & white movies starring Cary Grant or James Stuart to musicals to westerns to war films to Sci-Fi to Basil Rathbone Sherlock Holmes films. We would soak up every film we possibly could.

I remember fondly a few years later my sister babysitting and us both staying up to watch The Godfather whilst eating chips from the takeaway. We lasted up to the dead horse part.

So naturally there was always a John Wayne film on. My dad was a huge fan and consequently I became one too. Wayne was a true Hollywood star and also, before the time when Public Enemy told me he was a racist.

We would have Sunday roast and all crash out on the sofa watching one of his films on TV and the whole family would snooze to the gentle sounds of Wayne annihilating the Native American population.

So when I got the part of the Centurion in my school nativity play, Father was ecstatic because John Wayne had played the centurion in the 1969 John Huston film *'The Greatest Story Ever Told.'*

If you've been lucky enough not to see it don't worry. You've missed only 4 hours of turgid *Hollywoodised* biblical epic. It's an appalling film that has some amazing casting. Max Von Sydow is Jesus and Shelly Winters (she of Poseidon Adventure and Alfie fame) plays Mary Magdalene. John Wayne doesn't appear till the very end

when Jesus is on the cross. He walks in, sees Jesus on the cross and says, 'Aw surely He is the son of God."
Although with so many pauses it sounds like,
"Aw… Surely… He… Is… The… Son… of… God."
Legend has it that despite the one line of dialogue Wayne couldn't get it right. John Huston turned to him and said,
"That's brilliant John, brilliant. But it needs more reverence. It needs more awe!"
TAKE 2
"AWWWWWWWWWWWWWWW WWWWWWWE Truly… He… is… the … son… of… God!"
So I didn't have a lot of competition in the acting stakes.
Like John Wayne I too had only one line of dialogue, which was,
"Search the village, collect the children!"
This however was not good enough for Dad and so he changed it and coached me to do it in the voice of John

Wayne. He changed it to this,
"Well get in that village… and get me those kids!"
He even tried to get me to walk like John Wayne. For those of you who haven't seen a John Wayne film you should know that his primary acting muscles were his shoulders. Think Schwarzenegger but without the gravitas. He would put those shoulders forward and almost fall over with only some sort of gravity defying will preventing him from toppling over. I was 5 years old, I couldn't walk like John Wayne. I walked like Norman Wisdom. A drunk Norman Wisdom.
They gave me a centurion helmet, so large, that combined with my crap walk, wobbled on my head so much that when I stopped to deliver my line it fell to the floor. I promptly burst into tears and had to be carried out of the church hall by Dad as I screamed,
"BUT HE IS THE SON OF GOD DAD! HE IS! HE IS!"
On the plus side I was never forced to watch another John Wayne film again.

CHAPTER 2
JUST WHEN YOU THOUGHT IT WAS SAFE

In celebration of my acting debut (I say celebration, I think Mum had taken off for the afternoon and Dad didn't know what else to do.) Dad decided to take me to see my first film at the cinema.

I vividly remember driving past cinemas when I was younger, attracted by the posters and the titles. They looked like massive palaces to me and I was so excited to finally to be going to one and with my Dad. I can remember it so clearly even now. We went to our nearest one, the Streatham Odeon. I remember I was wearing shorts and got very excited when Dad bought some popcorn from an old lady behind the counter. She had a white shirt on that was partially covered by a vividly striped waistcoat. Her glasses were on a chain and hung just below her neckline.

Do you remember your first film at the cinema? Chances are it was probably a Disney film. Brilliant works designed to be perfectly safe entertainment for families with children.

It wasn't a Disney film.

Now my Dad as I've said was a naval man and consequently obsessed with all things to do with the sea. I was 5 so the choice to him was obvious.

He took me to see Jaws.

I'm sure you've seen Jaws. Pretty much everyone has. It is an amazingly good film with many great scenes. My particular favourite scene is the one where the 5-year-old child... is eaten by the shark.

I didn't sleep for a year.

Dad with his engineering brain however couldn't understand why I was having trouble separating reality from the film. To him it made no sense. Now, Dad being an educated man never missed the opportunity to pass on that knowledge at any available moment. So in order to help me get to sleep he gave me a lecture. A lecture that would prove how safe I was from Shark Attack, a lecture on the most common causes of death in 1976.

Number 1 Road traffic accident.

Number 2 Falls.

Number 3 Poisons.

He then ends this lecture with the now legendary sentence,

"SO YOU SEE. YOU'RE MORE LIKELY TO BE RUN OVER BY A BUS ON YOUR WAY TO SCHOOL TOMORROW MORNING... SLEEP WELL.

Needless to say this didn't help.

Now at this point in the show I wanted to show clips from the films in question. Unfortunately it costs a ridiculous amount of money in licensing to show clips so I had a solution. Being as how I'm a massive fan of film. I have a video camera, some friends and more importantly a dog, what could go wrong? Sadly not all my friends were on the same page as me.

Jaws Sketch

http://www.youtube.com/watch?v=798 jwxhcxsc

INT. REHEARSAL STUDIO DAY

4 rather lovely & brilliant comics stand around eating snacks and looking really annoyed.

ROB DUMBRELL

He thinks he's Steven Spielberg

RUE BARRATT

Yeah

SAM SAVAGE

He does, it's like he's living in a bubble. What's he doing?

RUE BARRATT

His mental state is disintegrating.

SAM SAVAGE

I don't like it when he cries when you tell him something he doesn't like. That's what gets me, that's why I don't want to do it. It's like kicking your Nan.

ROMESH RANGANATHAN

He's so needy.

RUE BARRATT

Like a child.

Off screen we hear

AIDAN(OS)

DUDES!

The camera spins round and we see Aidan standing at a table. He is holding up his jacket and behind it something moves. He starts to do the Jaws theme.

AIDAN

Da Dum. Da Dum. Dad dum dadum dadum dada!

He whips back the jacket to reveal…

His dog Kimble, a border terrier. Kimble has a cardboard shark fin attached to his back.

AIDAN(very enthusiastically)

It's the shark!

Cut back to the 4. They look massively unimpressed.

EXT. BRIGHTON BEACH DAY

Kimble sits next to Aidan as a ball is waved around.

AIDAN

See! He looks just like a shark!

Aidan throws the ball and Kimble chases after it. His shark fin wobbling as he runs towards the waves.

CUT TO: The 4 who are now standing on the beach.

RUE BARRATT

Shall we just go?

SAM SAVAGE

He's not going to notice.

They walk away.

CUT TO: Kimble, ball in mouth being trounced by a large wave.

END OF SKETCH

Now when I show this sketch people laugh. They laughed and then they feel sorry for my dog. This is a dog whose entire happiness is dependent on jumping in the sea on a daily basis regardless of weather. He is insane.

However stick a fin on him and film him and people look at you like you are evil, so here is a picture of him all safe and warm post-shoot in his trailer.

At this point in 1976 I should introduce my mother. She had of course been an integral part of the story so far (what with giving birth etc) but it was at this point that mother stepped in to divert a potential catastrophe. As a witness to Dad's lecture and seeing the look of total fear on my face, Mum did something that all mums do at some point in their child's life. She told a little white lie.

Now there's nothing wrong with this and if you think about it this happens all the time. Parents will tell little white lies to make you feel better about things. Like for example. The tooth fairy.

We all in our heart of hearts know that they don't exist but it's a lot nicer thinking that a mythical beastie will come down and reward you for your tooth, rather than standing there worried because part of you has fallen out of your head.

So my mum, thinking as quickly as she could, said the first thing she could think of. She after all was there when Dad was off around the world working. She was the one who'd have to deal with the late nights, the nightmares and the lack of sleep.

"Don't worry." She said "You'll always be perfectly safe as long as you always have your red wellies with you."

They were there at the door of my room. My red wellies. Now in fairness to Mum I think she meant that I should be safe with them being in close proximity. I instead chose to wear them. I wore them all the time. I wore them to school. I wore them to bed. I even wore them in the bath. Well you would. There's water in there and one thing we do know is that THERE ARE SHARKS IN THE WATER!

I even wore them when we went on holiday to Greece.

Apologies for the Sharon Stone pose.
There I was in the full heat of the Mediterranean sun wearing my red wellies and perfectly safe from shark attack. I also found the following picture, which confused me at first.
It is of me with my sister, yet you can see I am clearly upset by this and I think I know why.

There I am clearly distressed by something whilst standing next to me is my sister who I love very much but if you look closely you can see that while I am wearing my red wellies she is not.

AND IS THEREFORE DOOMED!

I have now reached adulthood and still to this day have a pair of red wellies with me at all times.

And I would like to point out that I have still yet to be attacked by a shark. So if you take nothing else away from this book then it should be always to listen to your mother. She knows stuff.

CHAPTER 3
DARTH VADER IS A WUSS

This wasn't in the show but I just
wanted to say something and
chronologically it fits in here. During
the show I wanted to say a bit about
Star Wars and not in a positive way. It
was pointed out to me (quite rightly)
that any stuff on Star Wars has been
done to death and would detract from
the show as it's not one of the films I
saw with Dad.

It's just that Darth Vader is a rubbish
Villain. There I've said it. He's a
cipher to represent the bad guy and cut
out from the most basic character arc
that fits the Star Wars story. Also any
credibility he had as a villain is totally
destroyed by the abomination that was
the Prequels. A series of films that
reduced a really bad guy into a

petulant teenage boy with mother
issues.

I know Star Wars has its many fans
and I don't blame them but my
feelings were not helped by having
recently seen the scariest villain in
movie history on TV mere days before
seeing the space epic.

The sad thing is that this character
rarely makes various top 10 lists but
should be because he makes Darth
look like a small boy who shouts
'Yippee' unconvincingly. (oh hang on
George Lucas did that already)

It's the character of Bill Sykes played
by Oliver Reed in the musical
'OLIVER.'

Yes you read that right. There in the
middle of a big Hollywood style
musical is the most convincing
portrayal of villainy ever. It's as
though the director had given Oliver a
different script to the one everyone
else has got. He is a brutal, murdering
thug who scared the living daylights
out of me when I saw him. His English
bull terrier 'Bullseye' only served to

show the merest form of humanity in the character and he just used his charisma to eat up the screen. Reed clearly terrifies all the other actors and gives his best ever performance. He also has one of the most exciting and bleak deaths in cinema ever. Check it out.

CHAPTER 4
HISTORY LESSONS

When it came to putting together this show I talked to my Dad and asked why we always went to the cinema. It was all we ever seemed to do. Any time we had a spare hour or two and were alone we went. We saw some brilliant films, one Saturday we went to the West End of London to watch '*Flash Gordon*' a film so camp it needed a soundtrack by Queen just to butch it up a bit, and we saw some dross too.

'*Popeye*' with Robin Williams was 2 hours that I'm still trying to get back and also ''*Krull*' a British fantasy film that had every British actor ever in it.

It holds a special place in my heart as being the first film I'd watched at the cinema and thinking 'Oh this is a bit rubbish isn't it?"

Of course I told Dad it was great. He said so too so I must've got it wrong. We talked enthusiastically about it on the way home and when we got back Mum asked Dad what he thought of it. Dad must've thought he was out of earshot because I remember he distinctly telling Mum it was 'Awful.'

I was too young too realise at the time the significance of this. We were at a stage in our relationship where to save any embarrassment we were prepared to lie to make each other happy: a barrier that had removed itself by the time we saw *'Return of the Jedi.''* I remember the horror in dad's voice when the Ewoks first appeared.

"OH GOD"

I felt his pain and even the Luke / Darth face off couldn't save us from the dire quality control. It was when the once mighty Chewbacca swung onto a Walker while singing out the Tarzan jungle call, I called it quits. The shark had jumped and so had our collective patience.

It was also the first time I had sworn in front of Dad.

"Dad, is it just me or is this utter shit?"

I remember Dad roared with laughter and then told me off for swearing.

It turns out that the reason for all this film watching was a result of Dad's own upbringing. Apparently all he ever did with his dad was go to the cinema to avoid conversation. Virtually twice a week Dad would be carted off to the cinema to watch films again and again. The earliest film Dad says he remembers seeing was the now classic World War 2 propaganda film *'Went the Day Well?'*

Consequently I've had to watch it with Dad about a million times and I still love it.

If you haven't seen it yet then you are missing out on an absolute classic. It stars Thora Hird amongst others, SHOOTING NAZIS!

Honestly, if you thought 'Songs of Praise' was her highpoint you haven't seen anything till you've seen Thora with a Webley shooting indiscriminately at the attacking enemy.

The plot concerns a group of German paratroopers who, disguised as English troops, have to capture and hold hostage an entire British village. A village by the way that is populated by the most frightfully plucky people you've ever met.

Now chances are you've seen plenty of films in which either the good guys or bad guys are in disguise and are rumbled by a simple thing they never accounted for. When doing the show comma at this point I always ask the audience if they can guess how the Germans are rumbled?

There have been many suggestions from accents to eating Bratwurst in public but none have ever got it right. Have a think, see if you can guess because I'm willing to bet unless you've seen the film you never will.

They are actually foiled by a bar of chocolate.

I'm not making this up. The scene is

an acting master class of understatement.

POSH WOMAN: "My that's odd. This bar of chocolate just fell out of Corporal Henderson's rucksack!"

POSH MAN: "Well what's so odd about that?"

POSH WOMAN: "Well it says…"

THERE IS NOW A PAUSE SO LONG YOU COULD FIT THE ENTIRE D DAY LANDINGS THROUGH IT.

POSH WOMAN: "It says Chocolade!"

POSH MAN: "But that's how they spell Chocolate in Germany. Why would Corporal Henderson have German chocolate…UNLESS!"

And from that they kill them all.

It's really put me off shopping at LIDL.

It does of course beg the question, since when has chocolate been a tool in major detective work?

http://www.youtube.com/watch?v=8hisKEkCSfs

INT. DINING ROOM EVENING

Black & white film.

We see the 4 suspects all sitting around the table at a dinner party. The Detective stands at one end opposite our view with two either side. From the angle of the camera we cannot see who is sitting just below us.

DETECTIVE
The reason why I've called you all here tonight is that I believe one of you...
In turn we cut to each dinner guest as they give best shock reactions to what the detective is saying.
DETECTIVE
... is a German spy!
All four instantly look shocked and turn to face each other and then look to camera.
CUT TO: The fifth guest is Kimble the dog who is eating from the plate in front of him. It is covered in sweets and chocolates.
(Those of you that are keen dog enthusiasts and are already calling the RSPCA fear not. The advantage of filming in black & white is that mini

sausages look a little like chocolates)

Now you'd think following that lesson and my own childhood I would have learned something wouldn't you?
I have a daughter called Rosie and if you have a child yourself you'll know a certain fact. By the time your child reaches the age of about 6, you begin to realise something. Something you never thought could happen. It's the cold hard fact that when if you have to watch another animation you're going to go absolutely bus stop mental.
The tempting lure of slightly more grown up films is just on the horizon and one day one of those films came on TV and I remember seeing it when I was roughly the same age as my daughter.
Dad of course took me to see the film. It was great. We loved it. We loved it so much that straight after Dad took me to a shop so I could get a jacket so I could look like the hero. Then shortly after Dad bought himself a hat so he could look like the hero.

Now the film never did me any harm so surely it would be perfectly acceptable to show my daughter '*Raiders of the Lost Ark?*'

Have you any idea how many people get shot in the head in that film? Obviously more than zero is too much for a 6 year old. I'd even made that classic mistake parents make when showing films and completely forgot about the melty face bit at the end but it was all right. We didn't have any nightmares because Rosie just laughed. Phew. All was OK.

Until the next day when I got a phone call from school telling me that during the lunch hour Rosie had removed her belt and was whipping Nazis heads off in the playground.

I had inadvertently created a 6-year-old Nazi hunter. Which in the long run I didn't think was such a bad thing. I walked away suitably chastised and thought nothing more of it until 3 weeks later the school was doing a production of '*The Sound of Music.*'

I have never been so scared in my life.

I sat there in sheer horror as my child, who was playing one of the infinite number of children of the Von Trapp family, (Primary school productions usually have multiple actors playing each part. It gives everyone a turn and keeps eager parents happy. It does however do nothing for making any sense of the narrative) arrived on stage. What would she do when the Nazis turned up? I needn't have worried because the school dealt with it brilliantly by cutting the Nazis out completely!

It became a rather turgid boring love story. At the end Rosie came up to me.

"Did you enjoy that daddy?"

"Yes, of course but it was a bit different from the film, as in the film, there are Nazis."

Rosie paused as she thought this last statement through and then her face lit up as she realised what this statement meant.

"Indiana Jones is in the sound of music!"

If you think about it that would quite

possibly be the best film ever.

CHAPTER 5
QUALITY TIME

I guess another reason why we may have had difficulty communicating was that Dad & I didn't really have a lot of quality time together. This was mostly due to Dad traveling around the globe on various engineering projects. There were however one thing that if Dad was in town we would always do and that was always on Thursday nights BBC2 at 6pm.

The 6pm slot on a weekday was the best moment for kids. Dinner and homework (yeah, right!) had been done and they had the best things on. Usually old black & white short films like Flash Gordon with Buster Crabbe or my personal favourite Basil Rathbone as Sherlock Holmes.

This was I think a golden time for television. There were only three channels, BBC's 1 & 2 and ITV and that was it. Satellite TV & the Internet had yet to beam in from the skies and Channel 4 was a long distant dream of teenage boys to come.

Rumour has it Channel 4 would be showing naughty foreign films late at night causing adolescent guys to stay up late into the night praying that erotica would soon be displayed. It's important to note that teenage boys at the time equated a brief flash of breasts in a French new wave film to be a naughty foreign film. I personally remember tuning in my black & white portable TV to Channel 4 one night with my headphones on, so as not to be found out by the parents. The film that I had cunningly deduced as being a total nudey fest was *Last Year at Marienbad'* which started at 11:45!

Surely this would be a winner, I mean it's French AND in Black & white. It was not. It's a series of beautifully shot sequences that have relatively no narrative connection to each other or to the characters in the scenes themselves and seems to be concerned about the ennui of existence and existential angst.

So you know, no tits.

In effect it's like watching 472 Calvin Klein commercials in a row while melting your brain with a blowtorch and replacing it with grilled Halloumi cheese.

However on Thursday nights at 6 would be the one splash of glorious vibrant colour in the form of one of the greatest TV shows ever made, STAR TREK!

Now whatever your opinion on Trek and it's followers it can not be denied that it's influence and storylines were groundbreaking for its time. Plus Kirk snogged Green women!

Dad and I loved it. We loved it because you always knew what you were going to get. You knew that every week Kirk would get into a ridiculous fight, McCoy would scream, "I'm a Doctor Jim, not a plumber/fighter/short order cook!" This would all end up of course with an epic space battle and lots of explosions. Epic stuff.

We also loved it because my mother is an English freak. I don't mean she's a member of the EDL or anything but that she is a devout lover of the English language and abhors any kind of grammatical error. (This book has been proof read but she'll undoubtedly find the deliberate mistakes I left in.*)

*Obviously not deliberate.

Her problem with Star Trek is that at the beginning Kirk famously says '...to boldly go...' which is splitting an infinitive. He doesn't need to say it. So when the show started Dad or I would lean over to the TV set and turn the volume up really loud so that we could hear mother explode from the other side of the house.

"WHY DON'T THEY JUST GO! THEY COULD BE BOLD WHEN THEY GET THERE!"

This obsession with the English language and grammar also extended to diction and so my sister and I were raised listening to Radio 4 in order to promote good annunciation. A skill that I quickly dropped after the first day of secondary school. One day in a south London comprehensive and I went from having a future reading the shipping forecast to possibly appearing as a convincing street urchin in the musical 'OLIVER.'

Although this cover was blown when up to some high jinks with my new found friends one day I ruined the effect by shouting,

"Lordy it's the Rozzers! We'll be done up like kippers unless we shift it lads."

Followed by a quick pirouette and full dance routine.

So when in 1979 *Star Trek: The Motion Picture* came out Dad and I were ecstatic. Surely this would be the best film ever. Star Trek on the big screen would trounce that young upstart and show it who was the bigger, badder and better boss. Star Wars was a simple tale that was entertaining enough (We had seen it with Mum at the Streatham Odeon. Twice in one day as Mum fell asleep during the first showing so we stayed for the next screening. Score) but it wouldn't have any of the excitement and adventure of this young upstart.

If you have seen it then you know that it is without doubt the longest most boring film in existence and I should know, I've seen 'Last Year at Marienbad.' It goes on so long that when I went in I was 8 years old. When I came out I'd missed my first wedding.

It was such a misfire of a film. It was actually directed by the same man, Robert Wise, who had directed 'THE SOUND OF MUSIC.' Never before have I watched a Sci-Fi epic and prayed for the Von Trapp family to turn up. By half way through (roughly 6 months) there had been no fights, no exploding spaceships and more importantly no green women. It was also sad to note that he best special effect in whole film was William Shatner's wig.

There were other times when we did try to have quality time together that didn't require films.

In 1983 a chap called Richard Noble broke the land speed record by driving very fast in a straight line in Nevada. In 1984 Dad won a competition to be driven around Brands Hatch racetrack by Richard Noble. In a Ferrari and I was going too!

We got down to Brands Hatch, which was having a Ferrari owner's club day, which gave Dad the perfect opportunity to explain every minuscule detail of the internal combustion engine, the history of the Ferrari family & the socio-political implications of the Italian Renaissance on modern day society. (When I said he knows everything, I wasn't joking.)

So we get to Brands Hatch, and are ushered into an awaiting 400i and Nobel starts the engine. He floors the accelerator and we fly down the first straight, get right to the first corner and then spin 480 degrees and end up in the barrier. Noble pulls up the handbrake, takes off his helmet and says,

"Hahahaha Terribly sorry but I'm not very good with corners!"

After that it seemed safer to stick with films.

CHAPTER 6
ACCEPTABLE CRYING

Having an engineer for a dad would sometimes be a major bonus. Sometimes Dad would take me with him. I remember once we were in Lisbon. An amazing city, we'd spent most of the day under the stern of a ship inspecting the propeller. It was just like that scene in *'Indiana Jones and the Last Crusade.'*

You know when they are fighting by the ship with the spinning propeller? It was just like that. Exactly the same. Well the propeller wasn't spinning at all and if truth were told Dad and I weren't fighting religious zealots and for that matter we never found the Holy Grail but apart from all that it was exactly the same.

So that evening we had some time to kill and Dad had finished lecturing me on the historical movements of Portugal's naval fleet and the success of its most famous navigators Vasco De Gamma, so unsurprisingly we decided to go and see a movie. Lisbon is staggeringly beautiful and its architecture dates back hundreds of years (undoubtedly helped by Portugal's neutral stance in WW2) and its cinemas are a delight. Converted theatres that still have their intricate gold embossed edging to their theatre boxes and upper circles.

When I went there seemed to be a tradition of showing films for many years. The year was 1984 and I could see massive painted billboards on top of buildings for films like '2001' and *The Thing'* in amongst new releases like *'Amadeus', 'Ghostbusters' and 'The Adventures of Buckaroo Banzai in the 5th Dimension.'* (Ok maybe not the last one but it was a real film out that year. It has Jeff Goldblum in it.

Consequently it is wonderfully random.)

I saw one billboard and being a young boy of 13 years of age it caught my eye. Now being 13 and interested in what all 13 year old boys who've stayed up late into the night to watch French films were interested in the image presented told me that although this was a film I needed to see, I might have a tough time persuading Dad.

The image was of a girl. She was wearing hot pants, fishnet stockings, what I later learnt was called a Basque, and a bowler hat. She looked hot.

As my mother had been coaching me through the power of good diction and Radio 4 I instantly worked out my strategy. I would deliver a clear and concise speech. It would be unequivocal in it's purpose and would state, nay demand, that the only course of action open to us as gentlemen travelers, and British ones at that, would be for us to proceed with all haste to yonder theatre to sample what delights it may have! I remember it clearly. One couldn't help but remember such a notable oratory delight. Forgive my indulgence but I shall relay the text of the speech word for word so that you may take solace that the future of the English language is safe.

"heydadi'mnotsureifyou'dwanttobutth ere'sthatfilmonoverthereitmaybegoodit maynotbutithinkireadareviewonceabou titanditsgotgunsinitlotsofgunsandcarch asesandexplosionsandprobablyfighterp lanesithinkthegirlisonlyonthepostertopr omoteitwhatdoyouthinkshallwegoi'ms ureitsreallygoodandthecarchasesaawes omeandthereslotsofexplosionsbutitcoul dbeshiti'mnotsurewhatdoyouthink?"

Surely the spirit of Shakespeare looked down from the heavens and smiled knowing that the language he loved so much was in safe hands?
Now for some reason this didn't work with Dad and he wasn't too keen on showing his son 'Cabaret.'
So instantly he saw a more suitable

film playing in the cinema next door and so we went to see *'Escape to Victory.'*

If you haven't seen this film then you are missing out on one of the most amazing and bizarre films ever made. For the benefit of those who haven't, let me take a moment to explain the plot.

The film stars Michael Caine as a former professional footballer who is now a prisoner of war.

Max Von Sydow plays the camp commandant, a man so obsessed with football that he instantly recognises Michael Caine and organises for all the other prisoners of war who were once professional footballers to come to his camp so he can form a team.

This includes, by the way, Pele.

He then organises a match between his allied team and the German national team in the Stade de France, in Paris in the middle of occupied France.

In the meantime the Goalkeeper and mastermind of the escape plan organises for the entire team to escape during the halftime break.

It gets to half time and the Germans lead 4-1. They are about to make their escape when foolishly one of the English real life footballers is given the most important line in the film.

"Hang on, I think we can win this."

They go back.

They draw level and with seconds to spare the Goalkeeper stops a penalty that would have provided victory for the Germans.

The crowd of French civilians are ecstatic and storm the pitch gathering up our team, including Pele, and while giving them their own clothes help the entire Allied football team to escape the stadium and make their way into occupied France and to freedom.

At this point I would like to point out that the goalkeeper and therefore mastermind of the escape plan, is played by Sylvester Stallone.

I'm not making this shit up people. This film REALLY happened.

Now maybe if you haven't seen the film my description may not have sold it to you. Out of 10 you may have given it a low number. Unfortunately you are wrong.

Escape to Victory is one of the most marvelously nutty films ever made. Yes it's a load of shit but it's glorious shit. By the time the Allies and Pele were making their way out of the stadium I was in floods of tears and I defy anyone else not to be. The lights came up and much to my surprise I saw that my dad had shed a tear too.

This scared me to death. This man in front of me wasn't just my dad he was indestructible. He was John Wayne in British form. I had once seen Dad accidently put a nail through part of his hand, take it out with his teeth and ask me to pass the sellotape to wrap it up with. He was a God.

"Dad, have you been crying?"

'IT'S ALRIGHT SON. THERE ARE THREE OCCASIONS WHEN IT'S PERFECTLY ACCEPTABLE FOR A GROWN MAN TO CRY. THE BIRTH OF A CHILD. THE DEATH OF A LOVED ONE."

Pause.

"OR DURING A SPORTS MOVIE!"

Consequently I watch any sports movie and I'm in floods. Yes I know that our heroes will overcome adversity and become winners in the end. Yes I know that this will happen and yet I still bawl my eyes out. This goes for any sports movie too from *'The Mighty Ducks'* to *'Major League'*, (Which in my humble opinion is the best one) I even cried at *'Tin Cup'* for Christ's sake and that's about GOLF!

Of all the bizarre plot points of the film though the one I often wonder about is how does the entire Allied football team, being lead by Michael Caine, escape from occupied France?

The following sketch helps if in your head (if you're not watching it online) you do a terrible Michael Caine impersonation and a stereotypical German one. (No offense meant to Mr Caine as I am a massive fan of his work and have watched every single one of his films. Even the ones he was clearly doing to pay the rent. My favourite quote from him came when he was asked if he remembered anything about the filming of JAWS 4? "No, but I remember the house it bought." Also no offense meant to any Germans reading this as the intentional destruction of your language is done only to replicate Hollywood's inaccuracies for anything other than their own language. A fact that was made clear to me when after years of learning all the dialogue in *'Die Hard'* a German friend looked at me perplexed when I attempted a joke that involved the supposed German for 'Shoot the glass!')

EXT. BORDER CONTROL DAY
Dressed in T-shirt and shorts MICHAEL CAINE approaches the control point where 2 guards are standing.
He passes over his papers.
GUARD 1
Comen ze here bitter?
MICHAEL CAINE

Yavol Herr Oberst.

GUARD 1

(Incomprehensible German)

MICHAEL CAINE

Yavol Herr Oberst.

GUARD 1

(Lots and lots of incomprehensible German)

MICHAEL CAINE

Yavol. Herr Oberst.

GUARD 1 returns the passport to MICHAEL CAINE

GUARD 2

Gut Luck!

MICHAEL CAINE pauses briefly then look at GUARD 2

MICHAEL CAINE

Danke.

He walks away and while he does so the guards exchange words which are subtitled as follows.

GUARD 1

Shame. I was sure he was an escaped prisoner of war.

GUARD 2

Not with that perfect accent.

Back in Lisbon, Dad's statement about crying at the birth of a child led to an obvious question about my own birth and I discovered something that I never knew before.

It turns out that I was late for my own birth. They had a due date and Dad with his engineering brain had calculated everything down to the last detail and had organised to take the day in question off. However I wasn't playing by his rules and was over a month late. This was really annoying Dad (Mothers response to this can not be written down for fear of the blasphemy laws) and so he engaged his engineering brain and came up with a plan to get me out of my mother.

He spent an extraordinary amount of money renting a 2-seat sports car. He then drove my mother at unrealistic speeds around Kent and scared her so much her waters broke. He then delivered her to Beckenham hospital and after a 20 minute conversation with one of the doctors there about

engine capacity (an old bedtime favourite of mine) escorted my mother to the maternity ward and was present at my birth at 3am. I asked Dad if he cried? There was a momentary glimpse of softness in his eyes, which hardened quickly as he said,
'WELL OF COURSE I DID. I WAS SUPPOSED TO HAVE THE CAR BACK BY FIVE. YOU COST ME A FORTUNE!"

CHAPTER 7
TECHNICAL ERRORS

One day Dad and I were supposed to go and see *'Top Gun,'* the Tom Cruise starring advert for the American Air Force and gayest film ever made. (If you haven't seen it check out on YouTube Quentin Tarantino's dissection of the film which gives a different perspective on being someone's 'wing man.')

Accidently though we went to see *'Aliens.'*

It really was an accident as it was an 18 rated film, I was only 15, and we took the wrong door at the Catford ABC and found ourselves in Sci-Fi heaven. It is a brilliant film. It also had the added bonus that I was too young to see it legally, a fact that my father dealt with by telling me,

"KEEP QUIET, NO ONE WILL NOTICE."

In his usually delicate tones. It didn't work though as we were thrown out of the cinema after half an hour because Dad had an embolism due to his engineering brain going into meltdown.

Many a film's chances of glory have been destroyed by my father's attention to detail. Take for example *'Master & Commander'* starring Russell Crowe, a film set on a naval boat during the reign of George the Third. Dad's review was distinct.

"QUITE GOOD BUT THEY GOT A FEW THINGS WRONG!"

It's set in 1776, how does he know?

Initially however *'Aliens'* worked its magic and impressed Dad no end with its clever use of props.

If you've seen the film remember the big gun that the good guys have that's attached to a chest piece? Well the chest piece is actually from a steady-cam unit, the gun itself is from a Spitfire and the triggering Mechanism is actually from a Kawasaki 750R.

I know this because me dad told me so. During the film.

"OH THAT'S VERY CLEVER THEY'VE HAD TO RECYCLE IN THE FUTURE AND THAT'S WHY THAT WORKS SO WELL. WELL DONE!"

My dad thanking the cinema screen did little to placate the audience.

"Dad! Shut up you're going to get us thrown out!"

"IT'S OK SON. I'M ONLY EXPLAINING IT ALL TO THE PEOPLE."

But then something happened 27 minutes into the film (if you have the special edition 43) and Dad exploded. If you look at the scene where the troops and Ripley are walking through the laboratory for the first time, there on a table behind them for all to see, is a Tefal Deep Fat Fryer.

Oh it's there. I know this because guess who spotted it?

"WHAT IS THAT DOING THERE? THAT IS A TEFAL DEEP FAT

FRYER. WHAT IS THAT DOING IN SPACE? THIS FILM IS SHIT!"

We were ejected rapidly to the delight of the other patrons.

I figure it was because of Dad's attention to detail, his engineering brain couldn't justify the appearance of the fryer and it spoiled it for him. I'm not sure what was more worrying. The fact that he was prepared to let its appearance spoil his enjoyment of the film or the fact that he knew the brand?

His later thesis on the subject entitled "Why No-One in Space Fries' failed to justify his outburst despite becoming essential reading for all NASA employees.

There is only one other time when my father's attention to detail failed him and that was at my wedding. To give you some background it should come as no doubt to you that I've had a number of different jobs in my lifetime. I've been a heating engineer, a General Manager of a garden centre and also a bouncer. No really, I was. In a gay nightclub.

I actually got the job foolishly trying to impress a young lady that worked there and as the only two straight people there, I fancied my chances.

After making my moves and charming her with the old Goatley magic (18 months of hanging around and watching from afar like a lovesick puppy I finally got to kiss her) she agreed to be my wife. The wedding was amazing; we had five drag queens, 3 transsexuals and several very nervous homophobic relatives.

The fabulous owners of the club set up the reception in the venue itself. The entrance was festooned with pictures of naked men, my great Aunt Edith, who was 84 at the time (and bear in mind this was 10 years ago) still wants to go back.

Now if you have a wedding coming up or in fact any kind of celebration. May I be so bold as to suggest that you can't do any better for your entertainment purposes than having a 6ft, Glaswegian, Cher impersonator.

Just pop along to a Glasgow karaoke night and ask a 64 year old heavy set local to sing 'Turn Back Time' and you get the picture.

I still get nightmares.

Not because of the singing you understand but because while she was warbling away, Dad wandered up to me and in his usual manner told me,

'YOU KNOW THE ADVANTAGE OF SITTING AT THE BACK IS, FROM HERE, CHER LOOKS QUITE HOT!"

CHAPTER 8
WELCOME TO THE OVERLOOK-ON-SEA

INT.   MASSIVE DESERTED HOTEL DAY

Silence fills the room as we see an enormous deserted room. Its epic size is dwarfed by the massive sweeping staircase that dominates it.

At its base are the usual amounts of hotel furniture, sofas, chairs and tables, awaiting guests to sit there waiting for friends and family.

We move around and notice a large table at the far end. It looks as though it has been moved there. Slightly out of place. A large chair, almost throne like sits empty next to it.

On the table is an old typewriter. Reams of paper sit next to it.

We change perspective and look at the room from the far end.

AIDAN dressed in a checked shirt and a corduroy dress and carrying a baseball bat enters the room.

He looks terrified.

His face seems to hold a thousand questions and all the answers look unpleasant.

He looks around keeping the bat up to him so that if anyone attacks he is ready.

He slowly, cautiously makes his way over to the table.

He approaches the typewriter.

We cannot see what he sees but instead register the confusion on his face. He rolls up the scroll and we finally see what has been written.

Row upon row it says the same thing.

ALL WORK AND NO PLAY MAKE KIMBLE A DULL DOG

AIDAN frantically looks at the ream of paper which again has the same words written in different orders all over it.

AIDAN'S frantic searching through the paper is suddenly stopped by a deathly howl of a hound.

SCENE ENDS.

Where's the scariest place you've ever seen a film? I find that unless a film is truly scary, a cinema will not bring about true fear. You're usually sitting there amongst friends with popcorn around so you know you are safe.

I once was left in the house on my own. The parents were out for the night and my sister was staying with a friend. I think I was 12. I was watching Alfred Hitchcock's 'Psycho' and was gripped.

After 30 minutes I'd moved the TV round so I could watch it in the relative safety of the kitchen as the patio doors in the living room could easily be breached by Norman Bates' psychotic mother.

The detective, Arboghast, was making his way upstairs towards certain doom. The tension built by the fabulous score by Bernard Hermann and the editing put the viewer on a knife-edge. He made it slowly to the top of the stairs when suddenly a door opened and…

The power went off.

A power cut.

I sat there terrified for over an hour holding a carving knife and a frying pan.

When power was restored the film has finished and I was busy turning on all of the lights in the house. My parents returned that night to find their son fast asleep in a house with the equivalent brightness of the sun and armed with pots and pans in case of attack.

This was still not the scariest place I have seen a film.

That honour falls to 'The Shining', which I saw, in complete darkness in the middle of the North Sea.

I was 16 and Dad had got me a summer job on a tanker ship. It was called Atlantic Superior and was owned by a Canadian shipping company and the crewmen were all Portuguese. The Captain was ex-military and wore his full uniform at all times despite now being in the merchant navy. One evening he exited his cabin to take the air wearing his pajamas that actually had epilates and captain stripes on them.

I was planted in the medical room being an offspring of the management. The crew instantly thought I was a company spy apart from the one Brit, a Scotsman called Eddie, under who's influence I learnt the best way to swear.

There was a TV room for the officers and one for the Crew. I was allowed to use the officer's room and one evening found it empty. I looked through the tapes which all seemed to be of an 'adult' nature and actually found one playing. I don't know why it had been left playing but within 30 seconds I had worked out the plot and turned it off.

So I found The Shining and put it on.

I have never been so transfixed and terrified in my entire life!

It was mesmerising and the tension

was incredible. 20 minutes in the 1st mate popped his head in the door, saw me, said something in Portuguese and left.

I had never felt more alone in my entire life.

Now the corridors of an empty ship look unnervingly like a hotel and I had to walk through them to get back to my room. I slept in the TV room and again left all the lights on.

The next day despite the language barrier I could tell there seemed to be some hostility with the crew. I asked Eddie if I was imagining it and he quickly told me what was wrong.

"Some F***** put that ***ing film on last night!"

I never auditioned for RADA but if they had been there I would've got a place right there and then.

"What film?"

"The f****ing c**** Shining b******ks"

Eddie went on to explain that at the beginning of their work tour somebody had put The Shining on and the

Portuguese had watched it and universally hated it. Apparently when the crew finishes work and are at sea there's very little they like better than relaxing watching certain films and the VHS player in the Officers room was connected to the TV's in the cabins of the crew.

I had disturbed porn night.

Luckily armed with a Film Studies O'Level and an interpretation of the works of Kubrick put me in the perfect position to explain how this seminal film was in fact far more than it's whole & I asked Eddie if he would help me explain to the crew that this film in fact had a lot going for it and they could all enjoy it on another level.

"Don't be a prick kid. There's nae tits in it."

I had obviously not picked up my father's ability to lecture with authority.

CHAPTER 9
A BIT OF HOLLYWOOD WITH EDDIE

If in London, our chosen venue for a lot of films we saw together was Leicester Square comma the hub of the glittering West End. Situated in the heart of London this busy square with massive cinema palaces on each side was a Mecca to me as not only could you see the big Hollywood films but often you'd see someone famous either attending a premiere or just watching a film.

The first time was when Dad and I had been to see *'Midnight Run'* an excellent film starring Robert DeNiro at the Empire.

The Empire Leicester Square is an enormous cinema and tickets are about the same price as a small house so to

go there was a big treat. As we exited
the screening we made our way to the
gents' toilet and I could see there
seemed to be a bit of a crowd building
up.

Now remember that generational thing
I was telling you about? I saw the
crowd and chose to go round it to find
a way into the toilets. Dad however
was made of sterner stuff and
obviously feeling that any impediment
for a gentleman to enter a bathroom
was an affront to Queen and country,
he ploughed on through the crowd.
From where I now found myself
directly in sight of the corridor to the
gents toilet and also had a good view
of my father's trilby and umbrella
battling through the crowds like Henry
II at Agincourt.

I looked to the corridor and saw the
biggest man I have ever seen exiting
the toilets. He resembled a Zeppelin on
steroids. Behind him I could make out
a smaller chap, tiny in fact, and behind
him another behemoth that I'm sure
had a mother who loved him.

But Dad was heading right towards
them.
Dad made it to the front of the
corridor, the crowd had seen the
Zeppelin brothers coming and their
small companion and got excited and a
hush spread.
Then Dad got to the front of the crowd
and continued down the corridor
bumping into the first giant.
'EXCUSE ME.' said Dad in what I
could tell was his polite voice.
He repeated the phrase with the other
two and keeping his head down he
proceeded to the toilets.
The effect of my father's booming
voice and his natural indignation that a
gentleman should be delayed in his
quest had an almost calming effect of
the giants. They glanced at each other
and then looked to their small friend to
see if he was ok. The little man shook
his head and then beamed a smile at
the crowd as though nothing had
happened.
The small guy was Eddie Murphy.
I went forward to the bathroom and

joining father at the urinals was then stunned when a person we didn't know started to talk. (This is a truly horrifying thing when this happens as conversations in toilets for men are strictly forbidden. The average man can't cope with a chat in an elevator let alone when he is attempting to pee and has his genitalia in his hands. Needless to say there is no conversation to be had with a man trying to pee in a lift, at this point conversation would truly be dead.)

The young man, obviously excited at having seen the diminutive Mr. Murphy couldn't contain himself.

"Hey, you know who that was don't ya? Eddie Murphy!"

"REALLY?" said Dad in a way that indicated that not only that he didn't care but also that he might just kill if the man said another word.

"Yeah!" said the young man oblivious to his impending doom. "I wonder what he was doing here?"

Dad finishing his business as he was, zipped himself up said,

"HAVING A PISS NO DOUBT."
It was a statement of the obvious that
still left the young man confused.

CHAPTER 10
HOMO-EROTICISM:
WITH A VENGEANCE!

The next film on my list is *'Die Hard.'* The best action movie ever made.

It is a superb film that was made in 1989 and was the first film of the genre that took an action hero and showed he should get the absolute hell beaten out of him. Up till then we had Arnie and Stallone killing 300 plus per movie and getting a few scratches but then we got Bruce, cracking wise and getting beaten up. Sure he still killed about 300 but he broke a few ribs while doing it.

It's a very manly film. If you were going to score it on a scale of 1 to 10 for testosterone it would score 16 and fail a drugs test. On the plus side it would win the Tour De France 7 times in a row.

It's so manly its testicles have dropped and it needs a shave before you put it in the DVD player.

I'm sure if you've seen it you'll agree with me.

It's therefore quite surprising when I tell people that *'Die Hard'* is in fact a gay love story.

Still with me?

Ok let's look at the semiotics of the film. Here we have a man in a vest, trapped in a situation he doesn't want to be in. A marriage that hasn't worked and is represented by the tower block that still has several layers to be finished. Unable to come to terms with his homosexuality and a sham marriage Bruce has to fight his way out.

Outside is his lover, the cop. A man who is impotent without his lover (he is unable to fire his weapon) and it is only when Bruce accepts his homosexuality and comes 'out' of the building that he is able once more to fire his weapon and…..

Ok I know it's rubbish but this was my degree dissertation. Seriously I did a degree in Scriptwriting, which means I am qualified in absolutely nothing but I can write nice stories about it.

I wrote my dissertation on 'Homoeroticism in the Action Movie' and called it 'DISSERTATION WITH A VENGEANCE!'

I wrote it purely to wind up Dad who still would have a slight heart attack at the mention of homosexuality in movies. I once mentioned the rumour that John Wayne was gay and he didn't talk to me for a week.

It's true though; I did do a degree in Scriptwriting not that anything I write will ever get made. Hollywood just pretty much does remakes now. They even remade *"Clash of the Titans'* an appalling remake of a classic (classic as in fondly remembered from our youth and Harry Harryhausen's animation is genius kind of classic) film. It was so bad even the trailer was awful. I'm a big fan of trailers and love the way a good one is constructed.

(My favourite of all time, and yes I realise how sad it is to have a favourite trailer, is for *'Comedian'* a Jerry Seinfeld documentary. Check it out online) Even the tagline for this film was bad.

A good tagline will make a film seem exciting. I remember the tagline for *'Goldeneye'* was 'You Know the Number!' A brilliant link into 007. The tagline for *'Die Hard2: Die Harder'* was 'They said lightening never strikes twice!' Yay, same film as last time!

The tagline for *'Clash of the Titans'* was this,

'TITANS WILL CLASH!'

And I've been stuck in retail for most of my life.

That may of course be that the scripts I wrote at Uni were far from popular with my tutors. For our final project the one parameter we had was that it must be a historical work. I chose to write a historical detective piece. It was called 'JESUS P.I.'

Every week our Lord Jesus Christ

would solve crimes, in a mysterious way.

'What's that you say? Missing Loaves?'

"Jesus come quick, they're getting away on that boat!"

"I doubt that very much." Said Jesus as he walked across water to bring the blackguards to justice.

Needless to say this didn't impress my tutors very much and I left University armed with a low degree in Scriptwriting and went out into the big wide world.

For a while I was a support worker looking after children with emotional and behavioral difficulties. Which means I spent most of my time being beaten up by 15 year olds.

Of course having a degree in Media I was soon to find my natural home, retail. For a while I was even the General Manager of a massive Garden Centre despite knowing nothing about plants or management. Dad was very proud. I didn't have the heart to tell him I spent most of the day asking people,

"So what do you think we should do?"

And then saying something about empowerment and how we should all learn from each other. I lasted 3 years until I was found out. Garden management's gain was acting's loss.

Although I did learn very important things from my degree. If you spend 5 years watching films then you'll pick up all sorts of information like how to hack into computers, hot-wire a car and of course how to fly a plane.

There are only three things that you need to know in order to fly a plane.

1/ What the joystick does?

2/ What the pedals do?

3/ Which dial to tap when the plane runs out of fuel?

Why do they do this? A tonne of money is thrown at these things and yet a simple tap will solve the problem?

INT. BOMBER PLANE NIGHT

The plane has been battered and bruised. The co-pilot is clearly dead and there is a fire raging in the rear of the plane. Things do not look good for our hero DAVID NIVEN as he talks to his true love on the radio.

DAVID NIVEN

Hello June. I'm terribly sorry but it doesn't look like I'm going to make it. Ginger's bought it and Tommy and Nigel are goners too. I've lost the starboard engine and the port one is in flames. Also I don't have enough fuel to climb up to clear the cliffs of Dover. Afraid I'm going to have to bail out.

JUNE(OS)

Oh my darling I'm sure you'll survive.

DAVID NIVEN

Problem is, dear, my parachute went up in flames over Bordeaux. I'm sorry dear but this really will be it my darling.

PAUSE

JUNE(OS)

Darling, have you tried tapping the fuel gauge?

DAVID NIVEN

Oh crikey no completely forgot.

DAVID NIVEN taps on the fuel gauge and the starboard engine springs to life.

He taps again and the co-pilot shakes his head awake and gives him the thumbs up.

DAVID NIVEN

It's worked darling!

(I would like to point out that my university has produced many top quality people in their chosen fields while I spent far too much time having fun and playing Playstation games with my fellow layabouts. One friend from Uni recently had lunch with Jack Nicholson in Jack Nicholson's house interviewing him because he's now one of the editors of the biggest and best film magazines, Empire)

As I write this I'm sitting in Brighton Library with half a coffee and an empty Snickers wrapper by my side and wondering whether I can claim that the tramp sitting to my left is just Robert DeNiro researching his next role. He isn't. I just asked)

CHAPTER 11
THE WORST FILM EVER MADE

Life moves on and after University it kind of got in the way (Dear Jen comma I mean in a massively positive way my darling xxx) of Dad and I going to the cinema. So it was quite a while until we got a chance to get to the cinema again and it was to see what could only be described as the worst film ever made.

'Avatar'

Yes I'm aware that it made more money than God and it was nominated for 642 Oscars but it is an appalling film and for those that haven't seen it yet I will tell you how to avoid the horrors of watching this horrible tosh.
First go to the shops and buy a tin of

Quality Street.

Go home and remove the blue ones.

Take the wrappers and place them over your eyes.

And then just watch *'Dances with Wolves.'*

It is the same film. They should have just called it Dances with Smurfs it's so similar. Its main message is that machines are bad and trees are good.

That's it really. Machines are bad and Trees are good.

FOR THREE HOURS!

I sat there in absolute fury as this dire mess of a movie unfolded and couldn't believe how enraptured people had been of it. I was however sure of one thing, Dad would be hating it too. Remember when I said that Dad knows everything there is to know about everything? I wasn't joking, he really does. He has three degrees in total.

One in Advanced Engineering, one in Advanced Mathematics and one in Chemisty.

This means he knows exactly how

something has gone wrong, how to fix it and also time travel.

So I was pretty sure I'd know Dads reaction to this nonsense. To give you an idea of how silly this film is, sorry this Oscar nominated film, specifically Best 'ORIGINAL' screenplay film is I should tell you briefly about it.

Humans and machines are bad, trees and blue aliens are good (although they do need to be saved by the white man hero which of course brings up a whole other debate) and humans are after a mineral that is only available on the blue people's planet.

The name of the mineral in this OSCAR NOMINATED script (and bear in mind I have a degree in scriptwriting and work currently in a pet store) is amazingly called UNOBTAINIUM.

Seriously.

Unobtainium.

I have never been angrier in my entire life.

How the hell did this get made let alone praised enough to get an Oscar nomination?

The only things stopping me from exploding there and then was the safe knowledge that Dad would be exploding too. After all this was the man that got us thrown out of *'Aliens'* because of a deep fat fryer. Unobtainium would surely be making him explode like Krakatoa!

"I THOUGHT IT WAS BRILLIANT!"

"WHAT!"

I exploded with rage. How was this possible? This was a man who had lived his life and had ruled mine by a set of parameters that were set in stone. It was a simple code and everything just followed suit. It was the natural way of things, everyone knew that you always wore matching colour belt and shoes, you never had ketchup with a steak and any massive inconsistency in a film rendered it pointless.

I was astounded. If I could I would have given him a lecture, produced a copy of the periodic table and asked him where, where on this table (the very tool he had lived his life by) was UNOBTAINIUM?

His reply?

'IT'S ONLY A MOVIE, SON'

I couldn't let that go. I just couldn't. So for the benefit of the show and my sanity I got on the phone and tried to get Dad to come down and talk about *'Avatar'*.

I don't think Dad was prepared to admit defeat with regards to that film. You see he may have mellowed slightly over the years but he has always been incredibly competitive and I think he realised I'd won about *'Avatar'*.

So his saying 'It's only a movie" was his way of winning, of not admitting defeat.

At that point I realised that I've never beaten him at anything. It's stupid I know but the John Wayne mentality that I'd been brought up with took over and I became determined to beat him at something, if only to have a finale for my show.

The amazing thing is that he's so bloody good at so many things I was going to have trouble beating him to anything.

It was then I had what alcoholics call a moment of clarity. If I did something he's never done before then surely I would have won. The very fact that he'd never given it a go would mean that I would win no matter what.

Genius Right?

So it became clear what I should do. I knew that Dad had never done any running so if I did a race it wouldn't matter where I came because I would still be better. That idiotic macho need to better my father got in the way of any logic. So I entered the Brighton Marathon.

Stupid Right?

Just in case you're wondering the Brighton marathon is still 26 miles. Just because it's in Brighton doesn't mean we get time off for wearing the Vegas showgirl outfits.

It is without doubt the stupidest thing I have ever done in my life. (And I once watched *'Ishtar'* of my own free will and liked it.)

I did no training whatsoever apart from buy a proper pair of trainers and do a 5K run with zero preparation. The 5K I managed to do in an appalling time of 32 minutes and managed to beat a 74 year old woman in the final straight. I say beat, I actually kicked her to the ground with 20 metres to go but a win is a win right?

So the day of the marathon was here and following age-old advice from my father in any endeavour I stood right at the back of the crowd.

My thinking being that if I started last,

it could only get better. How wrong I was as this picture I took at the 10-mile mark shows.

Don't be fooled I hadn't overtaken a single soul and I was in so much pain my hips had declared war on the rest of my body and were in danger of winning.

But I still couldn't give up. The John Wayne Macho gene was still kicking in and I had to prove a point. I vowed to make it to the finish and 9hours and 46 minutes after starting I virtually crawled to the end.

One of the attendants shouted

encouragement as I waddled by,

"Get to the end mate, the announcer will call your name and the crowd is still there!"

Brighton is an amazing city and I have never been more pleased to be a resident of it when I looked up to see hundreds of people still out and cheering the last of the latecomers as the announcer called out names.

It was then that I spotted him.

Amongst the crowd and surrounded by a bunch of guys, I later learnt were the Brighton Gay Mens Chorus, was my Dad. He had come to cheer me on and he had stayed to the bitter end.

It was then I knew my moment had come. This was the time I would finally win. I would finally get one up on this man. The man who was my hero, the living embodiment of John Wayne.

I picked up my pace to at least 1 mile an hour and heard the announcer call,

"AND COMING UP HERE WE CAN SEE AN AMAZING SIGHT..."

This was it. I was ready to win.

Unfortunately I didn't realise one important fact. In my quest for stupid glory I didn't realise at first that the announcer was not calling out for me but for a group of three Japanese students behind me.

They had constructed and carried a 20ft replica of the Bullet Train around the 26 miles for a Tsunami relief charity.

And they overtook me.

They got to the finish line and everyone went mental. The crowds, the announcer and also the Gay Mens Choir but not Dad. He stood there and waited for me to finish.

It was then I realised how stupid I had been. I mean I'm a grown man and here I was carrying on like some 15 year old desperate for attention, trying to win against a man who was only trying to find the best way to communicate with me.

I went over to him,

"Well Dad. What d'you think?"

"I THOUGHT IT WAS A DISGRACE!"

A bit harsh I thought.

Dad pointed to the Japanese train.

"THEY CLEARLY HAD AN AERODYNAMIC ADVANTAGE!"

CHAPTER 12
THE BEST MOVIE EVER MADE

We come to the last film of the show. (Not of Dad and me, as thankfully we still have been able to attend the cinema together. When I was a young boy I got into reading comics and specifically 2000AD so it was with great pleasure we went to see the film *'Dredd'* recently)

'The Blues Brothers' is in my mind the best film ever made and is my absolute favourite. It came out in the early eighties and didn't set the box office alight but by mid-decade it had become a cult classic and was being shown every Friday at the Baker Street Odeon. Dad took me to see it as he had heard how good a film it was.

It was awesome. It was a musical, a comedy, and it had car chases and an array of cameos like I had never seen, James Brown, Aretha Franklin & Ray Charles to name but a few. It blew me away, not just the film but the music too. I had never been exposed to this music before and afterwards I discovered that this was Dad's favourite type of music. He, of course, knew everything about it and we spent the journey home talking about the Blues from Robert Johnson to BB King.

It was great to be talking about something together. Sure it had started with films but it was a different subject for us.

We got home and Dad said,

"WELL SEEING AS THAT YOU SEEM TO LIKE THE BLUES SO MUCH. NEXT YEAR AS A TREAT, WHY DON'T WE GO TO CHICAGO AND LISTEN TO SOME BLUES!"

Wow. That would be incredible. So this was in 1986.

In 2001 we finally went.

That's my dad there standing with my identical thinner cousin. (It was over 10 years ago and my diet starts tomorrow. Honest)

This was the car he rented, a red Ford Mustang convertible. We were going on a road trip from Washington to Indianapolis to watch the Formula 1 Grand Prix. The blues was still with us both but our aim was to stop briefly in Chicago on the way.

The trip was eventful to say the least with Dad's specific itinerary we had a lot of miles to cover and God help us if we stayed in one place longer than 8 hours.

We unfortunately got lost at one point in Baltimore.

In the Hood.

For those of you unaware of the delights of Baltimore and if you haven't seen 'THE WIRE,' imagine the worst parts of hell and add automatic weapons.

Dad's instant response was to turn on the central locking comma stop and ask for directions.

"FROM THOSE YOUNG CHAPS OVER THERE!"

Believe me when I say this was the first and undoubtedly the last time a Baltimore street gang was referred to as 'Chaps.'

I needn't of worried though as we did indeed get the directions we needed from the chaps (who were fine once they realised we were English and not any threat) with the added bonus of some crack. From a lovely chap called 'Blood.'

As we drove away we were both relieved that all was ok and I laugh now about Dad's putting on the central locking on a convertible car.

So we made it to Chicago and as we

had the luxury of a whole day till we moved on. We decided to tour Chicago and it's movie locations.

Chicago is a magnificent city and as full and vibrant as you'd imagine it to be. It's located right next to Lake Michigan (If you're British forget any concept you may have of a lake in your head. This is a sea in anyone else's mind) so you have the wonderful sight of skyscrapers next to a beach.

We went to Union station so we could see the stairs where *'The Untouchables'* has its *'Battleship Potemkin'* inspired shoot out. It was quite something to stand mid-way on the steps, as commuters happily walked up the other side, while Dad took a picture of me pretending to be Kevin Costner reaching for the pram that was heading for doom at the bottom.

Dad then made me take a picture of him pretending to be Robert DeNiro despite my assurances that as DeNiro does not appear in that scene he'd have to pretend to be someone else. Dad then gave me a look that indicated that as he was paying for this trip that if he wanted to be DeNiro pulling a gun on the steps then he would be DeNiro pulling a gun on the steps.

We then went on the El train. I tried to get Dad to run underneath it pretending to be Gene Hackman in *'The French Connection'* but he wasn't having any of it.

So that evening we're in town and looking for a film to watch when Dad remembered his promise and said we should go and find some blues somewhere.

So we ended up in a place called 'The House of Blues' a massively cool blues venue owned by Dan Ackroyd, one of the stars of The Blues Brothers.

Needless to say this was the coolest evening ever. There I was with my Dad, in Chicago, watching a Blues player twanging away. How much cooler could this be?

The guy on stage was exceptionally cool and held the audience as he sang and played his heart out.

This couldn't get any better.

And then amazingly it did.

The player left the stage and the announcer came on.

"We're gonna have a little break now of 5 or 10 minutes but don't go anywhere because we have a special treat after... The Blues Brothers Band!"

Oh.

My.

God.

The crowd went absolutely nuts as did I. How amazing was this? What were the chances of this happening on the very day that Dad & I were there?

I turned to Dad and laughed and acted like a 5 year old. Wow this was just outstanding.

And that's when he told me that we weren't going to the Grand Prix. We never were. We were always coming to the House of Blues. You see the reason we didn't go in 1987 was that Dad couldn't afford it.

He had a dream of taking his son on an amazing road trip across America in a car.

Not just any car as it had to be a Ford Mustang convertible, a red one. So that he and his son could wear sunglasses and look cool as we travelled to the home of his favourite music. So he spent the next 15 years saving the money so that we could do the trip in the style he wanted to do it in. It was only when he found out that The Blues Brothers Band were reforming just for a special night that he knew this was now the time for us to go.

When he told me I was just blown away. To think that for 15 years he had kept this plan secret was just incredible. I didn't know how to react I wanted to hug him and tell him how my heart was bursting with love for him. How it always had and that I loved him.

But of course I couldn't because of the macho John Wayne bullshit that I'd been filled with since childhood.

So all I could do was turn to him and

say,
'THIS IS GREAT!"
And Dad turned to me. Took off his sunglasses and with tears in his eyes and in the softest tone I've ever heard him speak said,
"And I love you too."

That is the end of my story. I guess the moral if you want one is if there's someone you haven't seen in a while, it could be your mum or dad, 2nd cousin or just an old friend. Give them a call & maybe catch a movie together. You don't have to tell them you love them but it's always nice to be reminded.
Dad came to see the show and do you know what happened after?

He bought me this bike for my birthday!
Take that Chris Hardy, mines got orange wheels.

Take care,

Aid X

EXT. STAGE DOOR EVENING

Aidan exits the theatre and is now wearing a black trilby along with his black suit.
He puts on some sunglasses and walks forwards to this Car!

He gets into the car.

AIDAN
It's 5462 miles to Chicago. We've got a full tank of gas and half a packet of cigarettes. It's dark and I'm wearing sunglasses.

He turns and we see that he has been talking to Kimble who is also wearing a suit.

AIDAN
No, It's ok Kimble. We're on a

mission from God.

Aidan starts the car and our two heroes drive off into the night.

ACKNOWLEDGEMENTS

I'd like to thank Mum & Dad obviously for having me. Emma & Billie for being an inspiration. Jill Edwards for her guidance. Rob Dumbrell, Romesh Ranganathan, Rue Barratt & Sam Savage for being in the show via films.

Also thanks to all those who joined in but sadly ended up on the cutting room floor Sean McLoughlin, Jim Holland, Tim Watts, Bill Gleave, Kerry Herbert & Roz Ryan.

Katie Wells took the photo's on the front of Kimble and me.

Peter Buckley Hall, the PBH Free Fringe and The Voodoo Rooms, Edinburgh.

The exceptional cover design is by David Jordan

Thanks also to all the audiences that came to see the show and laughed.

Dave & Pauline for their support & love.

My lovely daughter Rosie for coming on the Edinburgh adventure and also of course, Kimble the dog who stole the show and still does every day.

Finally I'd like to thank and dedicate this book to my wife Jennie who is my best friend. Thank you for all the laughs.

As a fan of films I always love it when there's a little extra bit at the end of the film. Sadly with the show that really is the end, so here for your additional entertainment is the beginning of my first proper novel.

When the world is coming to an end and all hope is lost. The fate of our planet rests in the hands of a young detective, a social worker, a kebab shop owner and an 84-year-old ex-spy called Mrs Uckbourne. We don't know what will happen but we know we've only got until...

NEXT WEDNESDAY*

*AFTER LUNCH

Bob woke up. This didn't surprise him, as it was what he usually did most mornings at this time. In fact very little surprised Bob. It was one of the few qualities that he had. His unsurpriserbility. Since childhood his parents had been often vexed by his ability to remain unaffected by their efforts on his birthdays. Even the time when they had moved him during his sleep and had put him in a tent in the garden.

Not that Bob didn't know how to have fun. Don't get me wrong. Bob was a very fun bloke who had a reasonable amount of friends for someone of his age and was considered to be fun to have around. It's just that nothing came as a surprise to him.

He pulled the duvet out of the way and sat up. Another unsurprising day lay before him. Bathroom, work, drink in the evening and then back home for a cup of tea and then bed. It wasn't much but Bob enjoyed it.

Bob went over to the window and

pulled back his curtains and found much to his surprise, that he was surprised. He was surprised for two reasons. One that it wasn't the usual view that always greeted him and two because he realised that he had about two seconds left to live.

Now the view that always greeted Bob in the mornings was of his street and the woman in number thirty-seven who always seemed to be getting dressed at that time in the morning. Needless to say this started Bob's day off quite well. Especially as the woman at number thirty-seven had seemingly never thought about closing her curtains when getting changed. However this morning, Bob was greeted with the sight of a Roman Legion marching towards him. Well that and a boulder that had been launched by a catapult that was heading directly for him.

While not actually known for his mathematical genius Bob quickly calculated that he could either move at the speed of around seventy three miles an hour and get out of the way or he could just stand there and swear. He swore.

"Shit."

This was unusual because Bob never swore. For a brief second Bob wished that his final words had been something a bit more profound but he rationalised very quickly that life, especially his, was too short.

"Fu...."

The phone rang.
It did that.
A lot.

It couldn't be blamed. That was its job. People phoned, it rang but still Gary couldn't bring himself to like it. Gary gave this some thought. He wasn't sure if it was because he hated the phone itself or just the ring. He'd much preferred it when phones had dials and had a bell inside them but since everything had gone electronic you just got this digital blast. This wouldn't be so bad but Gary's phone was worse. His spoke to him.

"Gary, it's for you. Gary, I'm ringing. C'mon Gary pick me up. This hurts." The problem was that Gary's' phone was possessed. For some reason the spirit of his phones previous owner had decided to stay. Gary had asked him once why.

"Hammond?"

"Detective Hammond."

"Sorry, Detective Hammond?"

"Yes Gary."

"Why have you stayed here in this phone and not, like, you know, gone off to another astral plane or something?"

"Well Gary, It's just there comes a time in your life when you just realise that you never got the opportunity to be really useful, you know. I just felt that maybe if I stuck around for a bit then I could be of more use."

Needless to say Gary had thought about asking the phone, sorry, detective Hammond why he chose to help by possessing a phone but there never seemed to be the right opportunity. He knew that life as a police detective in the relatively inconsequential town of Sunbourne was far from riveting, but if he died Gary was sure that if he must come back as a phone then he'd chose one that a, was in a very busy area and b, was operated by a stunning woman who with any luck had what could only be described as a staggering cleavage.

Putting questions of his phones existential existence aside Gary picked up the receiver and tried to ignore the words of thanks that were emanating from it. It was an internal call from the Desk sergeant, Sarge. He had been at the desk for so long that no one was exactly sure as to what his real name was but he seemed happy to be called by his title. The police station in Sunbourne, like the town itself, was certainly a weird place and you had to forego the eccentricities that it's inhabitants displayed. The Sarge was unfortunately obsessed with using the internal phone system. Not so bad you may think but as the Sarge was only in the next room and that Sunbourne's police station had only three rooms and one of them doubled up as a kitchen/bathroom then his obsession seemed a bit strange. Especially as the door was always open. This led to any phone conversations coming through to Gary in a rough form of stereo. Which was lucky in itself, as the Sarge had the most monotonous voice in the world and anything that might make a conversation with the man less tedious tended to help.

"Yes" said Gary without putting the phone to his ear.

"There's been a suspicious death sir." droned the Sarge.

"Really?" said Gary " A real suspicious death or one like last year?"

"That could have been suspicious sir."

Gary remembered the death last year. An eighty-nine year old gent by the name of Albert Watkins had fallen down dead of seemingly natural causes in the local supermarket. The Sarge had become convinced that the man was killed by foul means. Gary had tried to explain to him that a man dying in the breakfast food aisle, although occurring around cereal did not mean that it was the work of a serial killer and his attempt to rectify the Sarges' baffling understanding of the English language fell on stony ground . The Sarge was not convinced and to this day felt that Gary should have investigated the matter further. Gary chose to ignore this point and let the Sarge give him the details of the suspicious death.

"What's suspicious about it then?"

"He was killed with a boulder, sir."

"A boulder?"

"Yes sir." said the Sarge so matter of factly that Gary was almost convinced that death by boulder was a regular occurrence.

Gary took the details and set off to investigate. Well he set off. Investigation was something that appeared on the television and certainly not in Sunbourne. Things just didn't happen there. Well things of a nature that required a police presence. Gary often wondered what he had done to be placed there.

He put it down to the one day in training when during a riot simulation Gary had tried to diffuse the situation by building a campfire and singing songs. Gary had passed the test purely on his singing ability but it was thought best for his own safety that he was given a nice safe assignment. So that is how Gary Pearson found himself at the rank of detective at the age of 28. He would have made the news due to the fact that he was the youngest police detective ever but the national press had tried to find Sunbourne and got lost on the way. Instead Gary's story appeared in a tabloid newspaper on page 14 underneath the weather report and next to a letter from a young lady who was concerned about her husbands' premature ejaculation. Gary had been quite proud of the newspaper clipping

and had stuck it on the wall.
Unfortunately the larger headline that
read " I WANT A MAN THAT CAN"
tended to get the wrong reaction from
visitors.

Gary got into his car. A very old Ford
Cortina that was considered racy by
Sunbourne standards. Mind you a snail
that felt the need to carry not only its
shell but a small aircraft carrier would
be considered racy.

It took Gary twenty minutes to travel
what would normally be a five-minute
drive anywhere else, because he was
stuck behind a caravan. Gary had seen
the caravan around before. In fact he
had never seen it parked up. It was as
though the driver was constantly
searching for one of the many caravan
parks that populated the region.

Gary got out of the car and made his
way into Bob's house. The ambulance
men were sitting around smoking and
looking very pale. In fact they looked
as though they would rather be sitting
at home and watching daytime TV.
Gary took this as a bad sign as most

people would rather have root canal work with no anesthetic than watch daytime TV.

Gary entered the room to see a rather large boulder sitting in the middle of the room. It actually looked quite peaceful, like a rather deformed coffee table. Gary was thinking that it might be difficult to balance a cup of coffee on it but it had a certain something. That something was the four limbs sticking out from underneath it.

Gary looked out at what was left of the window. Well it was more of a round hole now but from the debris that was lying around Gary could see that it did once have double-glazing. Very important that. Kept the draft out.

He looked at the limbs. He knew that the Sarge was right about this one. This was very suspicious and just a little weird.

Gary noticed something. There was no blood.

"Where's the blood?"

"Still in him I think." said Davis, Sunbornes' very own Doctor.

"Oh dear." said another ambulance
man as he dashed towards the door.
Gary went over to the window.
Outside he could see his car, the
ambulance and three of its attendants
all looking as though they would rather
be on This Morning.

On the other side he saw Number 37.
Gary was no stranger to trigonometry
as he had taken the subject at GCSE
and had had gained a grade 2.
Therefore he was pretty sure that the
bolder came from the kitchen of the
opposite house.
Coming out of the house Gary crossed
the street and walked over to the
house. There was no sign of any kind
of disturbance and no sign of anyone
who lived there.
There was nothing else for it.
He was left with no option.
He'd have to ask the Sarge to check the
Free Roaming Data Dispensing
Provider, (FRDDP).
20 minutes later after fumbling with a
pay phone while the Sarge checked in

the FRDDP or phone book, as it was more commonly known, Gary discovered that the occupant of No. 37 was a Miss Lucy Winters.

The planets rested in the ever-expanding swirl that was the Cosmos. In an area of one galaxy commonly known as the "Arse end of the Universe", (That is the part not called Uxbridge) an energy mass started to collect and form. The energy mass had been dormant for some time, though unaware of this the mass started to take its natural shape. That of a woman. The creator of all life stifled a yawn and vowed never to use the snooze button again. The effect of these infernal machines had caused many to oversleep. The creator of all life had overslept by about 50,000 years. This was the problem with being an immortal. The time just flew by. It wasn't as if she had just sat around for a bit. She'd actually achieved quite a lot. So there had been a few mistakes. Jupiter was supposed to have been a foot spa and she was beginning to become aware of a phenomenon known as a 'Fast Food Chicken Outlet.' This was another problem with being the Creator of all Life. Not only was she immortal she was also omnipresent and omnipotent. If she wanted to go somewhere she was already there and she knew everything that had happened. It really put the notion of holidays into perspective. No finding a charming little bistro while on holiday for her because she had not only created it but had also designed the menu.

Needless to say being a woman once a month she would suffer the same fate as all women. This was a bit of a mistake on her part. It was during the development process that she started the symptoms that would plague all women. She felt sorry for this technical glitch that she had inflicted on females. Many a cry she had heard from the female of species throughout the universe. She tried to amend the situation but was only reminded of it

once a month and at the time she
would find herself just all over the
place. One of the side effects of being
omnipresent and pre-menstrual.
Bummer.
She could of course go back in time
and change things as she saw fit. It
wasn't really time travel as we imagine
it. It was more like going back to
check you'd turned the cooker off
when you went out even though you
haven't left yet. It wasn't as if she
would meet herself there either as she
found that she was omnipresent at all
times. Even Bank holidays.
She needed a break. She decided that a
visit to her favorite place was in order.
An insignificant planet that contained
many life forms that were under the
illusion that they were far more
important than they actually were. As a
result of their audacious attitude the
Creator of all life decided to teach
them a lesson. She decided to leave
them alone and not interfere with their
way of life. Unfortunately she
instigated this plan before she realised

that these beings did not have the same lifespan as her, so they never really got the point. Hope though, always sprung eternal. Maybe one day they would understand. Actually she knew that the day in question would be June the 23rd in the year 2634. Another problem she suffered was that it was pretty tricky to surprise herself. Then again it wasn't as if there was any other omnipresent beings around who could surprise her. She drifted round the planet and entered the thoughts and minds of its inhabitants. It was when she passed over the Northern Hemisphere she began to notice something strange. In a small sea-side town events seemed to be taking place of a startling nature. They were startling because for the first time she didn't know what would happen.

The grass curled up around her pink tracksuit as she lay on the ground. She was at peace. She was perfectly relaxed. She was at one with the world. She was Eighty-Four.

She was Mrs Uckbourne.

Around her she could hear the sound of children playing and laughing. She looked down past her feet and saw the kids. There was about five of them. One of them seemed to glow in a weird way. Not evil, but certainly out of place.

Further away she could make out a man walking towards them. The children parted and the man approached Mrs Uckbourne. She could make out he was wearing a RAF uniform. She stood up and straightened out the pink tracksuit. She then turned around and held her arms out to the man. They embraced. It was Mr Uckbourne. He'd been dead since 1935.

"Hello Mrs Uckbourne."

"Hello Mr Uckbourne."

As they held each other she felt the years slip away. This was the moment she lived for. In every dream Albert would return and ask her to come with him. She didn't know where and she didn't know why. All she knew was that she wasn't ready yet. She declined once again his offer. They sat down next to each other and watched the children they never had, play.

The child that glowed slightly took it upon herself to disappear at this point. Reforming herself into her chosen form, The Creator of all life decided to leave Mrs Uckbourne to enjoy her peace and take a look around the town. Besides she knew that the doorbell was about to ring and disturb the old lady's sleep.

As Gary was still pondering the trajectory of the boulder and beginning to think that an evening class in advanced algebra might help, Lucy Winters was parking her car on the far side of town. She pulled up the hand brake and let out a long sigh. It was a sigh that could be interpreted in many ways. Most of those interpretations would be negative and they would be right. Lucy was worried about Mr. Collins and his leg.

Sunbourne was very popular with old people. They retired here to be by the sea and get away from the hustle and bustle of their working lives. They came by their hundreds. This meant that Sunbourne's only growth industry was care work.

It all started in 1872 when the ageing Lord Anthony Propwell, 32nd cousin to Queen Victoria, visited the town and declared that the fresh air and invigorating sea water had made him feel like a new man. This declaration was seized upon by the towns' folk and soon Sunbourne became a tourist haven. The fact that Lord Propwell was clinically insane and regularly declared that he was a new woman called Edith was glossed over as it was felt that advertising the fact that the bracing air and invigorating sea water was beneficial to men with gender identity crisis' would not help the tourist trade.

So Lucy Winters was kept very busy visiting the towns old folk and helping them with their lives. A smile formed on her face when she realised that Mr Collins and his leg was one of the downsides of her job. She was about to visit one of her more positive patients. In fact Mrs Uckbourne was probably the most positive.

After rising from her sleep Mrs Uckbourne answered the door and ushered Lucy in. Within minutes a large mug of tea and several sandwiches were placed in front of her, as was their now weekly routine. After the first few months of visiting the sprightly octogenarian Lucy soon realised that she undoubtedly got more from the experience than her gracious host, as Mrs Uckbourne filled the young care worker in on all the gossip that was going on.

Mrs Uckbourne had led a varied and exciting life but like most old people she didn't feel the need to brag endlessly about it. Instead she tended to marvel at the wonder of her new replacement hip and the freedom that it had brought back into her life. For the first few visits, Lucy had carried Mrs Uckbourne's case file with her but the vast collection of notes weighed as much as five bags of sugar and had started to give Lucy a bad back. So instead she took it home and occasionally read its detailed notes whenever she was feeling uninspired. Mrs Uckbourne's life had the effect of cheering up anyone who had heard it.

Mrs Uckbourne's husband, James, was a test pilot for the RAF who sadly died in a crash during the first year of their marriage in 1935. The distraught widowers grief was further compounded by the fact that the plane that he had been flying was so secret that his death was covered up and she was never allowed to even have a funeral for him. The cover up had been so extensive that when in September 1939 War was declared Call up papers arrived at Mrs Uckbourne's doorstep.

She looked at the papers for a long time and did what any right-minded patriot would do. She cut her hair, taped down her breasts and joined the RAF where she soon became embroiled in the Battle for Britain. Having shot down four German fighters and finding that several of her colleagues were rather worried about their feelings for their fellow comrade in arms, she was shot down over France. Finding her way through occupied territory she managed to hook up with the Resistance where her true identity was discovered and she was soon placed in Paris, where she gained the eye of an influential German Colonel and found herself working in the German high command. After several years of passing information back to Whitehall and rising up the ladder of her German employers, Mrs Uckbourne was transferred to Berlin where it was said that she worked in the upper echelons of the third Reich. Her time after the end of the war was shrouded in secrecy although it was believed that the Russians captured her where upon she found herself in the Kremlin. These were of course rumours that were never proved. Lucy had asked her boss once how Sunbourne social services had such detailed files on their residents. He had responded with a subtle wink and the statement "We have detailed files."

Lucy was distracted by Mrs Uckbourne returning from the kitchen with yet more sandwiches.

"I'm sorry?" said Lucy.

"My party. You are coming aren't you?"

There were many things in this world that Lucy could predict but one of them she couldn't would be a party at Mrs Uckbourne's. That should be something to look forward to and to dispel any thoughts of Mr Collins and his leg.

The creator of all life walked down the street and crossed over to join the crowd, narrowly avoiding being run over by a caravan that trundled past out of nowhere. There was a group of about fifty or so people milling around trying to look concerned and not quite so fascinated by the crane that had now arrived outside the house of Bob.

As she looked at the scene she realised that she was experiencing confusion for the first time. It was a weird feeling that gnawed at her insides at a constant rate. She knew little things. She knew that a boulder had killed a young man. She knew that the boulder had come from somewhere other than this time-line but as to why or how remained a mystery.

Looking back to the building she saw a young man exit from the house walking backwards and unravelling a large tape measure at the same time. She knew at that point that the young man was trying to work out the trajectory of the boulder. She was about to offer to help, as mathematics was one of her top hobbies when the young man stopped. Turned his head

over to the crowd and looked directly
at her. He smiled and then returned to
his backwards perambulation.
The creator of all life remained routed
to the spot. Terrified, worried,
confused and with a strange new
feeling in her stomach. It was then that
she realised that she had been
blushing.

After jotting down several notes in his
book and trying in vain to work out if
he'd made a mistake, Gary realised that
the boulder had come from within the
kitchen or the upstairs bathroom of
number 37. Well either of those two or
it had come from the direct result of a
Butterfly flapping its wings in China
and a freak Tsunami in the region of
Skegness. Gary vowed never to use
Chaos theory in his mathematics again.
As he stood there trying to make sense
of the days events two things stuck in
his mind. How could a boulder travel
from someone's kitchen, leave no
damage, killing a young man on the
other side of a street and who was that

woman he smiled at? There was clearly a lot of thinking that needed to be done and in Sunbourne when you needed to think there was only one place you went to. Gary knew that a visit to see Dennis was on the cards.

Rome wasn't built in a day. In fact it took many generations of labour to create the empire that spanned nearly the entire known world at the time. It was a fact that was greatly acknowledged by many great warriors and theologians, then and now. As the soldiers of the Roman Empire strode across Europe they knew in their hearts that the goal they sought may not happen within their lifetime or even the next. But still they marched on. To the north they traveled and to the east, west and south and met resistance wherever they went. It just took time that's all. It was this knowledge that General Lucidicus Julius told himself that very morning when the battle began.

Though he was not happy.

He was not happy for several reasons.

Firstly he had been promised the Germania campaign and he knew that the battle with the Goths of the North would bring himself, his family and the Empire great honour. He knew that the campaign would be his great mark on the world. He would be talked about for future generations as grandfathers sat with their grandchildren and told of the just but fair Roman general who led the soldiers bravely into war.
Secondly he missed his wife and kids. He had been traveling for over three months now and knew that the battle ahead could last for over a year. Then once the campaign had succeeded he would have to take control of the conquered land and govern it until Rome sent his replacement.
Thirdly he was not happy because this land that he stood upon did not feel right. There was no tension as he and

his troops landed. Usually there was a mass of locals stood upon the shoreline ready to fight to the death to protect the land that they loved. But this time there was no one except an old man who was walking a dog.

General Lucidicus Julius marched bravely to the frail old man and stood before him trying to ignore the dog that was sniffing where he shouldn't be.

"I am General Lucidicus Julius of the Roman Army, Chief standard bearer of the might of the Empire. And I have come to conquer this land and slay all who would stand in the way of the progress that is known as Rome!" said the General in his most conquering voice.

"That's nice." Said the old man. Who seemed to be more concerned as to the activities of his dog and why the big soldier hadn't attempted to shoo the animal away in that embarrassing way you have to when a pet is sniffing your crotch.

"Will you be staying long?"

Lucidicus had begun to wonder of it was such a good idea to let his second in command pick the landing spot, but he realised that it was his own fault for being sentimental when his Commander had said that it looked like a good spot for swimming.

The forth reason for his unhappy state truly baffled him. He had travelled far and had seen most things that would make any normal man quake in fear. He had witnessed the assault on the low lands of France. He had been in the thick of battle in Spain and had eaten at the restaurant owned by Romulus Donaculus (It doesn't matter what century you're in, fast food is always a risky business) but he had never seen anything like the events that had happened since the battle finally started this morning. To begin with the first boulder of the day had shot through the air in what seemed to be a perfect trajectory and had disappeared into thin air and then there was a flash of light. The light was so bright that the great soldier had to shield his eyes from its intensity. When he opened them he was a little perturbed to discover that he was no longer on the battlefield but in a strange place. A place which was very quiet and had peculiar buildings, but this was not disturbed him the most. It was when he saw a horseless carriage pulling a large white box behind it that his fear took hold of him. He ran and while he ran tried to wonder how quickly he could get back to Rome.

If you liked this and want to read more then please let me know via www.aidangoatley.com

Aidan Goatley is a stand up Comedian & Graduate of the Jill Edwards Comedy Workshops (www.jill-edwards.co.uk) He lives in Brighton with his wife, child, dog & a fish called Barry. His first solo show '10 Films with my Dad' was the word of mouth hit of the PBH Edinburgh Free Fringe 2012.

Kimble the dog now lives in Hollywood having signed a seven picture deal with Disney Studios and is set for a major role in the new Star Wars films and will be playing the part of Gin Took leader of the Ewok Freedom Fighters

Kimble appears courtesy of Disney